THE AMERICAN DREAM

Plays by EDWARD ALBEE

THE AMERICAN DREAM

A PLAY BY

EDWARD ALBEE

COWARD-McCANN, Inc. New York

For David Diamond

FIRST PERFORMANCE: January 24, 1961, New York City.
York Playhouse

PREFACE

The comments by the Messers Watts, Balliett, and Taubman, printed on the jacket of this book, while they are representative of a majority of critical reaction to *The American Dream*, do not tell the whole story. Naturally not. No sensible publisher will tout opinions antagonistic to his product. And while I have, in my brief (three years, five plays—two of them but fifteen minutes long) and happy time as a playwright, received enough good press to last me a lifetime, I would like to concern myself, here, with some of the bad—not because I am a masochist, but because I would like to point up, foolhardy though it may be of me, what I consider to be a misuse of the critical function in American press letters.

For example: The off-Broadway critic for one of New York's morning tabloids had his sensibilities (or something) so offended by the *content* of *The American Dream* that he refused to review the next play of mine that opened.

Another example: A couple of other critics (Bright Gentlemen who do their opinions for Intellectualist Weekly Sheets of—sadly, all in all—very small circulation) went all to pieces over the (to their mind) nihilist, immoral, defeatist *content* of the play. And so on.

May I submit that when a critic sets himself up as an arbiter of morality, a judge of the matter and not the manner of a work, he is no longer a critic; he is a censor.

And just what is the *content* of *The American Dream* (a comedy, yet) that so upsets these guardians of the public morality? The play is an examination of the American Scene, an attack on the substitution of artificial for real values in our society, a condemnation of complacency, cruelty, emasculation and vacuity; it is a stand against the fiction that everything in this slipping land of ours is peachy-keen.

Is the play offensive? I certainly hope so; it was my intention to offend—as well as amuse and entertain. Is it nihilist, immoral, defeatist? Well, to that let me answer that *The American Dream* is a picture of our time—as I see it, of course. Every honest work is a personal, private yowl, a statement of one individual's pleasure or pain; but I hope that *The American Dream* is something more than that. I hope that it transcends the personal and the private, and has something to do with the anguish of us all.

EDWARD ALBEE

New York City
May 24, 1961

THE AMERICAN DREAM
A *Play in One Scene* (1959–1960)

The Players: MOMMY
DADDY
GRANDMA
MRS. BARKER
YOUNG MAN

THE SCENE:

A living room. Two armchairs, one toward either side of the stage, facing each other diagonally out toward the audience. Against the rear wall, a sofa. A door, leading out from the apartment, in the rear wall, far stage-right. An archway, leading to other rooms, in the side wall, stage-left.

At the beginning, MOMMY *and* DADDY *are seated in the armchairs,* DADDY *in the armchair stage-left,* MOMMY *in the other.*

Curtain up. A silence. Then:

MOMMY

I don't know what can be keeping them.

DADDY

They're late, naturally.

MOMMY

Of course, they're late; it never fails.

DADDY

That's the way things are today, and there's nothing you can do about it.

MOMMY
You're quite right.

DADDY
When we took this apartment, they were quick enough to have me sign the lease; they were quick enough to take my check for two months' rent in advance . . .

MOMMY
And one month's security . . .

DADDY
. . . and one month's security. They were quick enough to check my references; they were quick enough about all that. But now! But now, try to get the icebox fixed, try to get the doorbell fixed, try to get the leak in the johnny fixed! Just try it . . . they aren't so quick about *that*.

MOMMY
Of course not; it never fails. People think they can get away with anything these days . . . and, of course they can. I went to buy a new hat yesterday.
        (*Pause*)
I said, I went to buy a new hat yesterday.

DADDY
Oh! Yes . . . yes.

MOMMY
Pay attention.

DADDY
I *am* paying attention, Mommy.

MOMMY

Well, be sure you do.

DADDY

Oh, I am.

MOMMY

All right, Daddy; now listen.

DADDY

I'm listening, Mommy.

MOMMY

You're sure!

DADDY

Yes . . . yes, I'm sure. I'm all ears.

MOMMY
(Giggles at the thought; then)
All right, now. I went to buy a new hat yesterday and
I said, "I'd like a new hat, please." And so, they showed
me a few hats, green ones and blue ones, and I didn't
like any of them, not one bit. What did I say? What did
I just say?

DADDY

You didn't like any of them, not one bit.

MOMMY

That's right; you just keep paying attention. And then
they showed me one that I did like. It was a lovely little
hat, and I said, "Oh, this is a lovely little hat; I'll take
this hat; oh my, it's lovely. What color is it?" And they

13

said, "Why, this is beige; isn't it a lovely little beige hat?"
And I said, "Oh, it's just lovely." And so, I bought it.
　　　(*Stops, looks at* DADDY)

DADDY
(*To show he is paying attention*)
And so you bought it.

MOMMY
And so I bought it, and I walked out of the store with the
hat right on my head, and I ran spang into the chairman
of our woman's club, and she said, "Oh, my dear, isn't
that a lovely little hat? Where did you get that lovely
little hat? It's the loveliest little hat; I've always wanted
a wheat-colored hat *myself*." And, I said, "Why, no, my
dear; this hat is beige; beige." And she laughed and
said, "Why no, my dear, that's a wheat-colored hat . . .
wheat. I know beige from wheat." And I said, "Well,
my dear, I know beige from wheat, too." What did I
say? What did I just say?

DADDY
(*Tonelessly*)
Well, my dear, I know beige from wheat, too.

MOMMY
That's right. And she laughed, and she said, "Well, my
dear, they certainly put one over on you. That's wheat
if I ever saw wheat. But it's lovely, just the same." And
then she walked off. She's a dreadful woman, you don't
know her; she has dreadful taste, two dreadful children,
a dreadful house, and an absolutely adorable husband
who sits in a wheel chair all the time. You don't know
him. You don't know anybody, do you? She's just a

14

dreadful woman, but she *is* chairman of our woman's club, so naturally I'm terribly fond of her. So, I went right back into the hat shop, and I said, "Look here; what do you mean selling me a hat that you say is beige, when it's wheat all the time . . . wheat! I can tell beige from wheat any day in the week, but not in this artificial light of yours." They have artificial light, Daddy.

DADDY

Have they!

MOMMY

And I said, "The minute I got outside I could tell that it wasn't a beige hat at all; it was a wheat hat." And they said to me, "How could you tell that when you had the hat on the top of your head?" Well, that made me angry, and so I made a scene right there; I screamed as hard as I could; I took my hat off and I threw it down on the counter, and oh, I made a terrible scene. I said, I made a terrible scene.

DADDY

(*Snapping to*)
Yes . . . yes . . . good for you!

MOMMY

And I made an absolutely terrible scene; and they became frightened, and they said, "Oh, madam; oh, madam." But I kept right on, and finally they admitted that they might have made a mistake; so they took my hat into the back, and then they came out again with a hat that looked exactly like it. I took one look at it, and I said, "This hat is wheat-colored; wheat." Well, of course, they said, "Oh, no, madam, this hat is beige; you go outside and see." So, I went outside, and lo and behold, it *was* beige. So I bought it.

DADDY
(*Clearing his throat*)
I would imagine that it was the same hat they tried to sell you before.

MOMMY
(*With a little laugh*)
Well, of course it was!

DADDY
That's the way things are today; you just can't get satisfaction; you just try.

MOMMY
Well, *I* got satisfaction.

DADDY
That's right, Mommy. *You did* get satisfaction, didn't you?

MOMMY
Why are they so late? I don't know what can be keeping them.

DADDY
I've been trying for two weeks to have the leak in the johnny fixed.

MOMMY
You can't get satisfaction; just try. *I* can get satisfaction, but you can't.

DADDY

I've been trying for two weeks and it isn't so much for my sake; I can always go to the club.

MOMMY

It isn't so much for my sake, either; I can always go shopping.

DADDY

It's really for Grandma's sake.

MOMMY

Of course it's for Grandma's sake. Grandma cries every time she goes to the johnny as it is; but now that it doesn't work it's even worse, it makes Grandma think she's getting feeble-headed.

DADDY

Grandma *is* getting feeble-headed.

MOMMY

Of course Grandma is getting feeble-headed, but not about her johnny-do's.

DADDY

No; that's true. I must have it fixed.

MOMMY

WHY are they so late? I don't know what can be keeping them.

DADDY

When they came here the first time, they were ten minutes early; they were quick enough about it then.

(*Enter* GRANDMA *from the archway, stage left. She is loaded down with boxes, large and small, neatly wrapped and tied.*)

MOMMY

Why Grandma, look at you! What *is* all that you're carrying?

GRANDMA

They're boxes. What do they look like?

MOMMY

Daddy! Look at Grandma; look at all the boxes she's carrying!

DADDY

My goodness, Grandma; look at all those boxes.

GRANDMA

Where'll I put them?

MOMMY

Heavens! I don't know. Whatever are they for?

GRANDMA

That's nobody's damn business.

MOMMY

Well, in that case, put them down next to Daddy; there.

GRANDMA

(*Dumping the boxes down, on and around* DADDY'S *feet*)

I sure wish you'd get the john fixed.

DADDY

Oh, I do wish they'd come and fix it. We hear you . . .
for hours . . . whimpering away. . . .

MOMMY

Daddy! What a terrible thing to say to Grandma!

GRANDMA

Yeah. For shame, talking to me that way.

DADDY

I'm sorry, Grandma.

MOMMY

Daddy's sorry, Grandma.

GRANDMA

Well, all right. In that case I'll go get the rest of the
boxes. I suppose I deserve being talked to that way.
I've gotten so old. Most people think that when you get
so old, you either freeze to death, or you burn up. But
you don't. When you get so old, all that happens is that
people talk to you that way.

DADDY

(*Contrite*)
I said I'm sorry, Grandma.

MOMMY

Daddy said he was sorry.

GRANDMA

Well, that's all that counts. People being sorry. Makes
you feel better; gives you a sense of dignity, and that's all

that's important . . . a sense of dignity. And it doesn't matter if you don't care, or not, either. You got to have a sense of dignity, even if you don't care, 'cause, if you don't have that, civilization's doomed.

MOMMY

You've been reading my book club selections again!

DADDY

How dare you read Mommy's book club selections, Grandma!

GRANDMA

Because I'm old! When you're old you gotta do something. When you get old, you can't talk to people because people snap at you. When you get so old, people talk to you that way. That's why you become deaf, so you won't be able to hear people talking to you that way. And that's why you go and hide under the covers in the big soft bed, so you won't feel the house shaking from people talking to you that way. That's why old people die, eventually. People talk to them that way. I've got to go and get the rest of the boxes.

(GRANDMA *exits*)

DADDY

Poor Grandma, I didn't mean to hurt her.

MOMMY

Don't you worry about it; Grandma doesn't know what she means.

DADDY

She knows what she says, though.

MOMMY

Don't you worry about it; she won't know that soon. I
love Grandma.

DADDY

I love her, too. Look how nicely she wrapped these
boxes.

MOMMY

Grandma has always wrapped boxes nicely. When I was
a little girl, I was very poor, and Grandma was very poor,
too, because Grandpa was in heaven. And every day,
when I went to school, Grandma used to wrap a box for
me, and I used to take it with me to school; and when
it was lunchtime, all the little boys and girls used to take
out their boxes of lunch, and they weren't wrapped nicely
at all, and they used to open them and eat their chicken
legs and chocolate cakes; and I used to say, "Oh, look
at my lovely lunch box; it's so nicely wrapped it would
break my heart to open it." And so, I wouldn't open it.

DADDY

Because it was empty.

MOMMY

Oh no. Grandma always filled it up, because she never
ate the dinner she cooked the evening before; she gave
me all her food for my lunch box the next day. After
school, I'd take the box back to Grandma, and she'd
open it and eat the chicken legs and chocolate cake that
was inside. Grandma used to say, "I love day-old cake."
That's where the expression day-old cake came from.
Grandma always ate everything a day late. I used to eat
all the other little boys' and girls' food at school, because

21

they thought my lunch box was empty. They thought my lunch box was empty, and that's why I wouldn't open it. They thought I suffered from the sin of pride, and since that made them better than me, they were very generous.

DADDY

You were a very deceitful little girl.

MOMMY

We were very poor! But then I married you, Daddy, and now we're very rich.

DADDY

Grandma isn't rich.

MOMMY

No, but you've been so good to Grandma she feels rich. She doesn't know you'd like to put her in a nursing home.

DADDY

I wouldn't!

MOMMY

Well, heaven knows, *I* would! I can't stand it, watching her do the cooking and the housework, polishing the silver, moving the furniture. . . .

DADDY

She likes to do that. She says it's the least she can do to earn her keep.

MOMMY

Well, she's right. You can't live off people. I can live

off you, because I married you. And aren't you lucky all I brought with me was Grandma. A lot of women I know would have brought their whole families to live off you. All I brought was Grandma. Grandma is all the family I have.

I feel very fortunate.

You should. I have a right to live off of you because I married you, and because I used to let you get on top of me and bump your uglies; and I have a right to all your money when you die. And when you do, Grandma and I can live by ourselves . . . if she's still here. Unless you have her put away in a nursing home.

I have no intention of putting her in a nursing home.

Well, I wish somebody would do something with her!

At any rate, you're very well provided for.

You're my sweet Daddy; that's very nice

I love my Mommy.
        (*Enter* GRANDMA *again, laden with more boxes*)

GRANDMA

(*Dumping the boxes on and around* DADDY's *feet*)
There; that's the lot of them.

DADDY

They're wrapped so nicely.

GRANDMA

(*To* DADDY)
You won't get on my sweet side that way . . .

MOMMY

Grandma!

GRANDMA

. . . telling me how nicely I wrap boxes. Not after what
you said: how I whimpered for hours. . . .

MOMMY

Grandma!

GRANDMA

(*To* MOMMY)
Shut up!
(*To* DADDY)
You don't have any feelings, that's what's wrong with
you. Old people make all sorts of noises, half of them
they can't help. Old people whimper, and cry, and belch,
and make great hollow rumbling sounds at the table; old
people wake up in the middle of the night screaming,
and find out they haven't even been asleep; and when old
people *are* asleep, they try to wake up, and they can't
. . . not for the longest time.

MOMMY

Homilies, homilies!

GRANDMA

And there's more, too.

DADDY

I'm really very sorry, Grandma.

GRANDMA

I know you are, Daddy; it's Mommy over there makes all the trouble. If you'd listened to me, you wouldn't have married her in the first place. She was a tramp and a trollop and a trull to boot, and she's no better now.

MOMMY

Grandma!

GRANDMA

(*To* MOMMY)
Shut up!
(*To* DADDY)
When she was no more than eight years old she used to climb up on my lap and say, in a sickening little voice, "When I gwo up, I'm going to mahwy a wich old man; I'm going to set my wittle were end right down in a tub o' butter, that's what I'm going to do." And I warned you, Daddy; I told you to stay away from her type. I told you to. I did.

MOMMY

You stop that! You're my mother, not his!

GRANDMA
I am?

DADDY
That's right, Grandma. Mommy's right.

GRANDMA
Well, how would you expect somebody as old as I am to remember a thing like that? You don't make allowances for people. I want an allowance. I want an allowance!

DADDY
All right, Grandma; I'll see to it.

MOMMY
Grandma! I'm ashamed of you.

GRANDMA
Humf! It's a fine time to say that. You should have gotten rid of me a long time ago if that's the way you feel. You should have had Daddy set me up in business somewhere . . . I could have gone into the fur business, or I could have been a singer. But no; not you. You wanted me around so you could sleep in my room when Daddy got fresh. But now it isn't important, because Daddy doesn't want to get fresh with you any more, and I don't blame him. You'd rather sleep with me, wouldn't you, Daddy?

MOMMY
Daddy doesn't want to sleep with anyone. Daddy's been sick.

DADDY

I've been sick. I don't even want to sleep in the apartment.

MOMMY

You see? I told you.

DADDY

I just want to get everything over with.

MOMMY

That's right. Why are they so late? Why can't they get here on time?

GRANDMA

(*An owl*)
Who? Who? . . . Who? Who?

MOMMY

You know, Grandma.

GRANDMA

No, I don't.

MOMMY

Well, it doesn't really matter whether you do or not.

DADDY

Is that true?

MOMMY

Oh, more or less. Look how pretty Grandma wrapped these boxes.

GRANDMA

I didn't really like wrapping them; it hurt my fingers, and it frightened me. But it had to be done.

MOMMY

Why, Grandma?

GRANDMA

None of your damn business.

MOMMY

Go to bed.

GRANDMA

I don't want to go to bed. I just got up. I want to stay here and watch. Besides . . .

MOMMY

Go to bed.

DADDY

Let her stay up, Mommy; it isn't noon yet.

GRANDMA

I want to watch; besides . . .

DADDY

Let her watch, Mommy.

MOMMY

Well all right, you can watch; but don't you dare say a word.

GRANDMA

Old people are very good at listening; old people don't like to talk; old people have colitis and lavender perfume. Now I'm going to be quiet.

DADDY

She never mentioned she wanted to be a singer.

MOMMY

Oh, I forgot to tell you, but it was ages ago.
            (*The doorbell rings*)
Oh, goodness! Here they are!

GRANDMA

Who? Who?

MOMMY

Oh, just some people.

GRANDMA

The van people? Is it the van people? Have you finally done it? Have you called the van people to come and take me away?

DADDY

Of course not, Grandma!

GRANDMA

Oh, don't be too sure. She'd have you carted off too, if she thought she could get away with it.

MOMMY

Pay no attention to her, Daddy.
            (*An aside to* GRANDMA)

My God, you're ungrateful!
> (*The doorbell rings again*)

DADDY

> (*Wringing his hands*)

Oh dear; oh dear.

MOMMY

> (*Still to* GRANDMA)

Just you wait; I'll fix your wagon.
> (*Now, to* DADDY)

Well, go let them in Daddy. What are you waiting for?

DADDY

I think we should talk about it some more. Maybe we've been hasty . . . a little hasty, perhaps.
> (*Doorbell rings again*)

I'd like to talk about it some more.

MOMMY

There's no need. You made up your mind; you were firm; you were masculine and decisive.

DADDY

We might consider the pros and the . . .

MOMMY

I won't argue with you; it has to be done; you were right. Open the door.

DADDY

But I'm not sure that . . .

MOMMY

Open the door.

30

Was I firm about it?

MOMMY

Oh, so firm; so firm.

DADDY

And was I decisive?

MOMMY

SO decisive! Oh, I shivered.

DADDY

And masculine? Was I really masculine?

MOMMY

Oh, Daddy, you were so masculine; I shivered and fainted.

GRANDMA

Shivered and fainted, did she? Humf!

MOMMY

You be quiet.

GRANDMA

Old people have a right to talk to themselves; it doesn't hurt the gums, and it's comforting.
(*Doorbell rings again*)

DADDY

I shall now open the door.

MOMMY

WHAT a masculine Daddy! Isn't he a masculine
Daddy?

GRANDMA

Don't expect me to say anything. Old people are obscene.

MOMMY

Some of your opinions aren't so bad. You know that?

DADDY

(*Backing off from the door*)
Maybe we can send them away.

MOMMY

Oh, look at you! You're turning into jelly; you're inde-
cisive; you're a woman.

DADDY

All right. Watch me now; I'm going to open the door.
Watch. Watch!

MOMMY

We're watching; we're watching.

GRANDMA

I'm not.

DADDY

Watch now; it's opening.
        (*He opens the door*)
It's open!
        (MRS. BARKER *steps into the room*)
Here they are!

MOMMY

Here they are!

GRANDMA

Where?

DADDY

Come in. You're late. But, of course, we expected you to
be late; we were saying that we expected you to be late.

MOMMY

Daddy, don't be rude! We were saying that you just
can't get satisfaction these days, and we were talking
about you, of course. Won't you come in?

MRS. BARKER

Thank you. I don't mind if I do.

MOMMY

We're very glad that you're here, late as you are. You do
remember us, don't you? You were here once before.
I'm Mommy, and this is Daddy, and that's Grandma,
doddering there in the corner.

MRS. BARKER

Hello, Mommy; hello, Daddy; and hello there, Grandma.

DADDY

Now that you're here, I don't suppose you could go away
and maybe come back some other time.

MRS. BARKER

Oh no; we're much too efficient for that. I said, hello
there, Grandma.

33

MOMMY
Speak to them, Grandma.

GRANDMA
I don't see them.

DADDY
For shame, Grandma; they're here.

MRS. BARKER
Yes, we're here, Grandma. I'm Mrs. Barker. I remember you; don't you remember me?

GRANDMA
I don't recall. Maybe you were younger, or something.

MOMMY
Grandma! What a terrible thing to say!

MRS. BARKER
Oh now, don't scold her, Mommy; for all she knows she may be right.

DADDY
Uh . . . Mrs. Barker, is it? Won't you sit down?

MRS. BARKER
I don't mind if I do.

MOMMY
Would you like a cigarette, and a drink, and would you like to cross your legs?

MRS. BARKER

You forget yourself, Mommy; I'm a professional woman. But I will cross my legs.

DADDY

Yes, make yourself comfortable.

MRS. BARKER

I don't mind if I do.

GRANDMA

Are they still here?

MOMMY

Be quiet, Grandma.

MRS. BARKER

Oh, we're still here. My, what an unattractive apartment you have!

MOMMY

Yes, but you don't know what a trouble it is. Let me tell you . . .

DADDY

I was saying to Mommy . . .

MRS. BARKER

Yes, I know. I was listening outside.

DADDY

About the icebox, and . . . the doorbell . . . and the . . .

MRS. BARKER

. . . and the johnny. Yes, we're very efficient; we have to know everything in our work.

DADDY

Exactly what do you do?

MOMMY

Yes, what is your work?

MRS. BARKER

Well, my dear, for one thing, I'm chairman of your woman's club.

MOMMY

Don't be ridiculous. I was talking to the chairman of my woman's club just yester— Why, so you are. You remember, Daddy, the lady I was telling you about? The lady with the husband who sits in the *swing?* Don't you remember?

DADDY

No . . . no. . . .

MOMMY

Of course you do. I'm so sorry, Mrs. Barker. I would have known you anywhere, except in this artificial light. And look! You have a hat just like the one I bought yesterday.

MRS. BARKER
(*With a little laugh*)
No, not really; this hat is cream.

36

MOMMY

Well, my dear, that may look like a cream hat to you, but
I can . . .

MRS. BARKER

Now, now; you seem to forget who I am.

MOMMY

Yes, I do, don't I? Are you sure you're comfortable?
Won't you take off your dress?

MRS. BARKER

I don't mind if I do.
(*She removes her dress*)

MOMMY

There. You must feel a great deal more comfortable.

MRS. BARKER

Well, I certainly *look* a great deal more comfortable.

DADDY

I'm going to blush and giggle.

MOMMY

Daddy's going to blush and giggle.

MRS. BARKER

(*Pulling the hem of her slip above her knees*)
You're lucky to have such a man for a husband.

MOMMY

Oh, don't I know it!

37

DADDY

I just blushed and giggled and went sticky wet.

MOMMY

Isn't Daddy a caution, Mrs. Barker?

MRS. BARKER

Maybe if I smoked . . . ?

MOMMY

Oh, that isn't necessary.

MRS. BARKER

I don't mind if I do.

MOMMY

No; no, don't. Really.

MRS. BARKER

I don't mind . . .

MOMMY

I won't have you smoking in my house, and that's that!
You're a professional woman.

DADDY

Grandma drinks AND smokes; don't you, Grandma?

GRANDMA

No.

MOMMY

Well, now, Mrs. Barker; suppose you tell us why you're
here.

GRANDMA
(*As* MOMMY *walks through the boxes*)
The boxes . . . the boxes . . .

MOMMY
Be quiet, Grandma.

DADDY
What did you say, Grandma?

GRANDMA
(*As* MOMMY *steps on several of the boxes*)
The boxes, damn it!

MRS. BARKER
Boxes; she said boxes. She mentioned the boxes.

DADDY
What about the boxes, Grandma? Maybe Mrs. Barker
is here because of the boxes. Is that what you meant,
Grandma?

GRANDMA
I don't know if that's what I meant or not. It's certainly
not what I *thought* I meant.

DADDY
Grandma is of the opinion that . . .

MRS. BARKER
Can we assume that the boxes are for us? I mean, can
we assume that you had us come here for the boxes?

MOMMY
Are you in the habit of receiving boxes?

39

United States Senator; but now . . . why now he's changed his mind, and for the rest of his life he's going to want to be Governor . . . it would be nearer the apartment, you know.

MRS. BARKER

You *are* fortunate, Daddy.

DADDY

Yes, indeed; except that I get these qualms now and then, definite ones.

MRS. BARKER

Well, it's just a matter of things settling; you're like an old house.

MOMMY

Why Daddy, thank Mrs. Barker.

DADDY

Thank you.

MRS. BARKER

Ambition! That's the ticket. I have a brother who's very much like you, Daddy . . . ambitious. Of course, he's a great deal younger than you; he's even younger than I am . . . if such a thing is possible. He runs a little newspaper. Just a little newspaper . . . but he runs it. He's chief cook and bottle washer of that little newspaper, which he calls *The Village Idiot*. He has such a sense of humor; he's so self-deprecating, so modest. And he'd never admit it himself, but he *is* the Village Idiot.

42

Oh, I think that's just grand. Don't you think so, Daddy?

Yes, just grand.

My brother's a dear man, and he has a dear little wife, whom he loves, dearly. He loves her so much he just can't get a sentence out without mentioning her. He wants everybody to know he's married. He's really a stickler on that point; he can't be introduced to anybody and say hello without adding, "Of course, I'm married." As far as I'm concerned, he's the chief exponent of Woman Love in this whole country; he's even been written up in psychiatric journals because of it.

Indeed!

Isn't that lovely.

Oh, I think so. There's too much woman hatred in this country, and that's a fact.

Oh, I don't know.

Oh, I think that's just grand. Don't you think so, Daddy?

DADDY

Yes, just grand.

GRANDMA

In case anybody's interested . . .

MOMMY

Be quiet, Grandma.

GRANDMA

Nuts!

MOMMY

Oh, Mrs. Barker, you *must* forgive Grandma. She's rural.

MRS. BARKER

I don't mind if I do.

DADDY

Maybe Grandma has something to say.

MOMMY

Nonsense. Old people have nothing to say; and if old people *did* have something to say, nobody would listen to them.

(*To* GRANDMA)

You see? I can pull that stuff just as easy as you can.

GRANDMA

Well, you got the rhythm, but you don't really have the quality. Besides, you're middle-aged.

MOMMY

I'm proud of it!

44

GRANDMA

Look. I'll show you how it's really done. Middle-aged people think they can do anything, but the truth is that middle-aged people can't do most things as well as they used to. Middle-aged people think they're special because they're like everybody else. We live in the age of deformity. You see? Rhythm *and* content. You'll learn.

DADDY

I do wish I weren't surrounded by women; I'd like some men around here.

MRS. BARKER

You can say that again!

GRANDMA

I don't hardly count as a woman, so can I say my piece?

MOMMY

Go on. Jabber away.

GRANDMA

It's very simple; the fact is, these boxes don't have anything to do with why this good lady is come to call. Now, if you're interested in knowing why these boxes *are* here . . .

DADDY

I'm sure that must be all very true, Grandma, but what does it have to do with why . . . pardon me, what is that name again?

MRS. BARKER

Mrs. Barker.

45

DADDY

Exactly. What does it have to do with why . . . that name again?

MRS. BARKER

Mrs. Barker.

DADDY

Precisely. What does it have to do with why what's-her-name is here?

MOMMY

They're here because we asked them.

MRS. BARKER

Yes. That's why.

GRANDMA

Now if you're interested in knowing why these boxes *are* here . . .

MOMMY

Well, nobody *is* interested!

GRANDMA

You can be as snippety as you like for all the good it'll do you.

DADDY

You two will have to stop arguing.

MOMMY

I don't argue with her.

46

DADDY

It will just have to stop.

MOMMY

Well, why don't you call a van and have her taken away?

GRANDMA

Don't bother; there's no need.

DADDY

No, now, perhaps I can go away myself. . . .

MOMMY

Well, one or the other; the way things are now it's impossible. In the first place, it's too crowded in this apartment.
(*To* GRANDMA)
And it's you that takes up all the space, with your enema
bottles, and your Pekinese, and God-only-knows-what-
else . . . and now all these boxes. . . .

GRANDMA

These boxes are . . .

MRS. BARKER

I've never heard of enema *bottles*. . . .

GRANDMA

She means enema bags, but she doesn't know the difference. Mommy comes from extremely bad stock. And
besides, when Mommy was born . . . well, it was a
difficult delivery, and she had a head shaped like a
banana.

47

You ungrateful— Daddy? Daddy, you see how ungrateful she is after all these years, after all the things we've done for her?

(*To* GRANDMA)

One of these days you're going away in a van; that's what's what's going to happen to you!

GRANDMA

Do tell!

MRS. BARKER

Like a banana?

GRANDMA

Yup, just like a banana.

MRS. BARKER

My word!

MOMMY

You stop listening to her; she'll say anything. Just the other night she called Daddy a hedgehog.

MRS. BARKER

She didn't!

GRANDMA

That's right, baby; you stick up for me.

MOMMY

I don't know where she gets the words; on the television, maybe.

MRS. BARKER

Did you really call him a hedgehog?

GRANDMA

Oh look; what difference does it make whether I did or not?

DADDY

Grandma's right. Leave Grandma alone.

MOMMY

(To DADDY)
How dare you!

GRANDMA

Oh, leave her alone, Daddy; the kid's all mixed up.

MOMMY

You see? I told you. It's all those television shows. Daddy, you go right into Grandma's room and take her television and shake all the tubes loose.

DADDY

Don't mention tubes to me.

MOMMY

Oh! Mommy forgot!
(To MRS. BARKER)
Daddy has tubes now, where he used to have tracts.

MRS. BARKER

Is that a fact!

49

GRANDMA

I know why this dear lady is here.

MOMMY

You be still.

MRS. BARKER

Oh, I do wish you'd tell me.

MOMMY

No! No! That wouldn't be fair at all.

DADDY

Besides, she knows why she's here; she's here because we called them.

MRS. BARKER

La! But that still leaves me puzzled. I know I'm here because you called us, but I'm such a busy girl, with this committee and that committee, and the Responsible Citizens Activities I indulge in.

MOMMY

Oh my; busy, busy.

MRS. BARKER

Yes, indeed. So I'm afraid you'll have to give me some help.

MOMMY

Oh, no. No, you must be mistaken. I can't believe we asked you here to give you any help. With the way taxes are these days, and the way you can't get satisfaction in ANYTHING . . . no, I don't believe so.

50

And if you need help . . . why, I should think you'd apply for a Fulbright Scholarship. . . .

MOMMY

And if not that . . . why, then a Guggenheim Fellowship. . . .

GRANDMA

Oh, come on; why not shoot the works and try for the Prix de Rome.
(*Under her breath to* MOMMY *and* DADDY)
Beasts!

MRS. BARKER

Oh, what a jolly family. But let me think. I'm knee-deep in work these days; there's the Ladies' Auxiliary Air Raid Committee, for one thing; how do you feel about air raids?

MOMMY

Oh, I'd say we're hostile.

DADDY

Yes, definitely; we're hostile.

MRS. BARKER

Then, you'll be no help there. There's too much hostility in the world these days as it is; but I'll not badger you! There's a surfeit of badgers as well.

GRANDMA

While we're at it, there's been a run on old people, too. The Department of Agriculture, or maybe it wasn't the

Department of Agriculture—anyway, it was some department that's run by a girl—put out figures showing that ninety per cent of the adult population of the country is over eighty years old . . . or eighty per cent is over ninety years old . . .

MOMMY

You're such a liar! You just finished saying that everyone is middle-aged.

GRANDMA

I'm just telling you what the government says . . . that doesn't have anything to do with what . . .

MOMMY

It's that television! Daddy, go break her television.

GRANDMA

You won't find it.

DADDY
(*Wearily getting up*)
If I must . . . I must.

MOMMY

And don't step on the Pekinese; it's blind.

DADDY

It may be blind, but Daddy isn't.
(*He exits, through the archway, stage left*)

GRANDMA

You won't find *it*, either.

Oh, I'm so fortunate to have such a husband. Just think: I could have a husband who was poor, or argumentative, or a husband who sat in a wheel chair all day . . . OOOOHHHH! *What* have I said? What *have* I said?

GRANDMA

You said you could have a husband who sat in a wheel . . .

MOMMY

I'm mortified! I could die! I could cut my tongue out! I could . . .

MRS. BARKER
(Forcing a smile)
Oh, now . . . now . . . don't think about it . . .

MOMMY

I could . . . why, I could . . .

MRS. BARKER

. . . don't think about it . . . really. . . .

MOMMY

You're quite right. I won't think about it, and that way I'll forget that I ever said it, and that way it will be all right.
(Pause)
There . . . I've forgotten. Well, now, now that Daddy is out of the room we can have some girl talk.

MRS. BARKER

I'm not sure that I . . .

MOMMY

You *do* want to have some girl talk, don't you?

MRS. BARKER

I was going to say I'm not sure that I wouldn't care for a glass of water. I feel a little faint.

MOMMY

Grandma, go get Mrs. Barker a glass of water.

GRANDMA

Go get it yourself. I quit.

MOMMY

Grandma loves to do little things around the house; it gives her a false sense of security.

GRANDMA

I quit! I'm through!

MOMMY

Now, you be a good Grandma, or you know what will happen to you. You'll be taken away in a van.

GRANDMA

You don't frighten me. I'm too old to be frightened. Besides . . .

MOMMY

WELL! I'll tend to you later. I'll hide your teeth . . . I'll . . .

GRANDMA

Everything's hidden.

MRS. BARKER

I *am* going to faint. I *am*.

MOMMY

Good heavens! I'll go myself.
(*As she exits, through the archway, stage-left*)
I'll fix you, Grandma. I'll take care of you later.
(*She exits*)

GRANDMA

Oh, go soak your head.
(*To* MRS. BARKER)
Well, dearie, how do you feel?

MRS. BARKER

A little better, I think. Yes, much better, thank you,
Grandma.

GRANDMA

That's good.

MRS. BARKER

But . . . I feel so lost . . . not knowing why I'm here
. . . and, on top of it, they say I was here before.

GRANDMA

Well, you were. You weren't *here*, exactly, because
we've moved around a lot, from one apartment to another, up and down the social ladder like mice, if you
like similes.

MRS. BARKER

I don't . . . particularly.

55

Well, then, I'm sorry.

MRS. BARKER
(*Suddenly*)
Grandma, I feel I can trust you.

GRANDMA
Don't be too sure; it's every man for himself around this place. . . .

MRS. BARKER
Oh . . . is it? Nonetheless, I really do feel that I can trust you. *Please* tell me why they called and asked us to come. I implore you!

GRANDMA
Oh my; that feels good. It's been so long since anybody implored me. Do it again. Implore me some more.

MRS. BARKER
You're your daughter's mother, all right!

GRANDMA
Oh, I don't mean to be hard. If you won't implore me, then beg me, or ask me, or entreat me . . . just anything like that.

MRS. BARKER
You're a dreadful old woman!

GRANDMA
You'll understand some day. Please!

Oh, for heaven's sake! . . . I implore you . . . I beg
you . . . I beseech you!

GRANDMA

Beseech! Oh, that's the nicest word I've heard in ages.
You're a dear, sweet woman. . . . You . . . beseech
. . . me. I can't resist that.

MRS. BARKER

Well, then . . . please tell me why they asked us to
come.

GRANDMA

Well, I'll give you a hint. That's the best I can do, because I'm a muddleheaded old woman. Now listen, because it's important. Once upon a time, not too very
long ago, but a long enough time ago . . . oh, about
twenty years ago . . . there was a man very much like
Daddy, and a woman very much like Mommy, who were
married to each other, very much like Mommy and
Daddy are married to each other; and they lived in an
apartment very much like one that's very much like this
one, and they lived there with an old woman who was
very much like yours truly, only younger, because it was
some time ago; in fact, they were all somewhat younger.

MRS. BARKER

How fascinating!

GRANDMA

Now, at the same time, there was a dear lady very much
like you, only younger then, who did all sorts of Good
Works. . . . And one of the Good Works this dear lady

did was in something very much like a volunteer capacity for an organization very much like the Bye-Bye Adoption Service, which is nearby and which was run by a terribly deaf old lady very much like the Miss Bye-Bye who runs the Bye-Bye Adoption Service nearby.

How enthralling!

Well, be that as it may. Nonetheless, one afternoon this man, who was very much like Daddy, and this woman who was very much like Mommy came to see this dear lady who did all the Good Works, who was very much like you, dear, and they were very sad and very hopeful, and they cried and smiled and bit their fingers, and they said all the most intimate things.

How spellbinding! What did they say?

Well, it was very sweet. The woman, who was very much like Mommy, said that she and the man who was very much like Daddy had never been blessed with anything very much like a bumble of joy.

A what?

A bumble; a bumble of joy.

Oh, like bundle.

Well, yes; very much like it. Bundle, bumble; who cares? At any rate, the woman, who was very much like Mommy, said that they wanted a bumble of their own, but that the man, who was very much like Daddy, couldn't have a bumble; and the man, who was very much like Daddy, said that yes, they had wanted a bumble of their own, but that the woman, who was very much like Mommy, couldn't have one, and that now they wanted to buy something very much like a bumble.

How engrossing!

Yes. And the dear lady, who was very much like you, said something that was very much like, "Oh, what a shame; but take heart . . . I think we have just the bumble *for* you." And, well, the lady, who was very much like Mommy, and the man, who was very much like Daddy, cried and smiled and bit their fingers, and said some more intimate things, which were totally irrelevant but which were pretty hot stuff, and so the dear lady, who was very much like you, and who had something very much like a penchant for pornography, listened with something very much like enthusiasm. "Whee," she said. "Whoooopeeeeee!" But that's beside the point.

I suppose *so*. But how gripping!

Anyway . . . they *bought* something very much like a

bumble, and they took it away with them. But . . .
things didn't work out very well.

MRS. BARKER

You mean there was trouble?

GRANDMA

You got it.
   (*With a glance through the archway*)
But, I'm going to have to speed up now because I think
I'm leaving soon.

MRS. BARKER

Oh. Are you really?

GRANDMA

Yup.

MRS. BARKER

But old people don't go anywhere; they're either taken
places, or put places.

GRANDMA

Well, this old person is different. Anyway . . . things
started going badly.

MRS. BARKER

Oh yes. Yes.

GRANDMA

Weeeeellll . . . in the first place, it turned out the
bumble didn't look like either one of its parents. That
was enough of a blow, but things got worse. One night,
it cried its heart out, if you can imagine such a thing.

60

MRS. BARKER

Cried its heart out! Well!

GRANDMA

But that was only the beginning. Then it turned out it only had eyes for its Daddy.

MRS. BARKER

For its Daddy! Why, any self-respecting woman would have gouged those eyes right out of its head.

GRANDMA

Well, she did. That's exactly what she did. But then, it kept its nose up in the air.

MRS. BARKER

Ufggh! How disgusting!

GRANDMA

That's what they thought. But *then*, it began to develop an interest in its you-know-what.

MRS. BARKER

In its you-know-what! Well! I hope they cut its hands off at the wrists!

GRANDMA

Well, yes, they did that eventually. But first, they cut off its you-know-what.

MRS. BARKER

A much better idea!

GRANDMA

That's what they thought. But after they cut off its you-know-what, it *still* put its hands under the covers, *looking* for its you-know-what. So, finally, they *had* to cut off its hands at the wrists.

MRS. BARKER

Naturally!

GRANDMA

And it was such a resentful bumble. Why, one day it called its Mommy a dirty name.

MRS. BARKER

Well, I hope they cut its tongue out!

GRANDMA

Of course. And then, as it got bigger, they found out all sorts of terrible things about it, like: it didn't have a head on its shoulders, it had no guts, it was spineless, its feet were made of clay . . . just dreadful things.

MRS. BARKER

Dreadful!

GRANDMA

So you can understand how they became discouraged.

MRS. BARKER

I certainly can! And what did they do?

GRANDMA

What did they do? Well, for the last straw, it finally up and died; and you can imagine how *that* made them feel, their having paid for it, and all. So, they called up the lady who sold them the bumble in the first place and told her to come right over to their apartment. They wanted satisfaction; they wanted their money back. That's what they wanted.

MRS. BARKER

My, my, my.

GRANDMA

How do you like *them* apples?

MRS. BARKER

My, my, my.

DADDY

(*Off stage*)
Mommy! I can't find Grandma's television, and I can't find the Pekinese, either.

MOMMY

(*Off stage*)
Isn't that funny! And I can't find the water.

GRANDMA

Heh, heh, heh. I told them everything was hidden.

MRS. BARKER

Did you hide the water, too?

GRANDMA

(*Puzzled*)
No. No, I didn't do *that*.

63

DADDY

(*Off stage*)

The truth of the matter is, I can't even find Grandma's room.

GRANDMA

Heh, heh, heh.

MRS. BARKER

My! You certainly did hide things, didn't you?

GRANDMA

Sure, kid, sure.

MOMMY

(*Sticking her head in the room*)

Did you ever hear of such a thing, Grandma? Daddy can't find your television, and he can't find the Pekinese, and the truth of the matter is he can't even find your room.

GRANDMA

I told you. I hid everything.

MOMMY

Nonsense, Grandma! Just wait until I get my hands on you. You're a troublemaker . . . that's what you are.

GRANDMA

Well, I'll be out of here pretty soon, baby.

MOMMY

Oh, you don't know how right you are! Daddy's been wanting to send you away for a long time now, but I've

64

been restraining him. I'll tell you one thing, though
. . . I'm getting sick and tired of this fighting, and I
might just let him have his way. Then you'll see what'll
happen. Away you'll go; in a van, too. I'll let Daddy call
the van man.

GRANDMA

I'm way ahead of you.

MOMMY

How can you be so old and so smug at the same time?
You have no sense of proportion.

GRANDMA

You just answered your own question.

MOMMY

Mrs. Barker, I'd much rather you came into the kitchen
for that glass of water, what with Grandma out here, and
all.

MRS. BARKER

I don't see what Grandma has to do with it; and besides,
I don't think you're very polite.

MOMMY

You seem to forget that you're a guest in this house . . .

GRANDMA

Apartment!

MOMMY

Apartment! And that you're a professional woman. So,
if you'll be so good as to come into the kitchen, I'll be

more than happy to show you where the water is, and where the glass is, and then you can put two and two together, if you're clever enough.

(*She vanishes*)

MRS. BARKER

(*After a moment's consideration*)
I suppose she's right.

GRANDMA

Well, that's how it is when people call you up and ask you over to do something for them.

MRS. BARKER

I suppose you're right, too. Well, Grandma, it's been very nice talking to you.

GRANDMA

And I've enjoyed listening. Say, don't tell Mommy or Daddy that I gave you that hint, will you?

MRS. BARKER

Oh, dear me, the hint! I'd forgotten about it, if you can imagine such a thing. No, I won't breathe a word of it to them.

GRANDMA

I don't know if it helped you any . . .

MRS. BARKER

I can't tell, yet. I'll have to . . . what *is* the word I want? . . . I'll have to relate it . . . that's it . . . I'll have to relate it to certain things that I *know*, and . . . draw . . . conclusions. . . . What I'll really have to do

66

is to see if it applies to anything. I mean, after all, I *do* do volunteer work for an adoption service, but it isn't very much *like* the Bye-Bye Adoption Service . . . it *is* the Bye-Bye Adoption Service . . . and while I can remember Mommy and Daddy coming to see me, oh, about twenty years ago, about buying a bumble, I can't quite remember anyone very much *like* Mommy and Daddy coming to see me about buying a bumble. Don't you see? It really presents quite a problem. . . . I'll have to think about it . . . mull it . . . but at any rate, it was truly first-class of you to try to help me. Oh, will you still be here after I've had my drink of water?

GRANDMA

Probably . . . I'm not as spry as I used to be.

MRS. BARKER

Oh. Well, I won't say good-by then.

GRANDMA

No. Don't.
    (MRS. BARKER *exits through the archway*)
People don't say good-by to old people because they think they'll frighten them. Lordy! If they only knew how awful "hello" and "my, you're looking chipper" sounded, they wouldn't say those things either. The truth is, there isn't much you *can* say to old people that doesn't sound just terrible.
    (*The doorbell rings*)
Come on in!
    (*The* YOUNG MAN *enters.* GRANDMA *looks him over*)
Well, now, aren't you a breath of fresh air!

YOUNG MAN

Hello there.

GRANDMA

My, my, my. Are you the van man?

YOUNG MAN

The what?

GRANDMA

The van man. The van man. Are you come to take me away?

YOUNG MAN

I don't know what you're talking about.

GRANDMA

Oh.
 (*Pause*)
Well.
 (*Pause*)
My, my, aren't you something!

YOUNG MAN

Hm?

GRANDMA

I said, my, my, aren't you something.

YOUNG MAN

Oh. Thank you.

GRANDMA

You don't sound very enthusiastic.

68

YOUNG MAN

Oh, I'm . . . I'm used to it.

GRANDMA

Yup . . . yup. You know, if I were about a hundred and fifty years younger I could go for you.

YOUNG MAN

Yes, I imagine so.

GRANDMA

Unh-hunh . . . will you look at those muscles!

YOUNG MAN

(*Flexing his muscles*)
Yes, they're quite good, aren't they?

GRANDMA

Boy, they sure are. They natural?

YOUNG MAN

Well the basic structure was there, but I've done some work, too . . . you know, in a gym.

GRANDMA

I'll bet you have. You ought to be in the movies, boy.

YOUNG MAN

I know.

GRANDMA

Yup! Right up there on the old silver screen. But I suppose you've heard that before.

YOUNG MAN
Yes, I have.

GRANDMA

You ought to try out for them . . . the movies.

YOUNG MAN

Well, actually, I may have a career there yet. I've lived out on the West Coast almost all my life . . . and I've met a few people who . . . might be able to help me. I'm not in too much of a hurry, though. I'm almost as young as I look.

GRANDMA

Oh, that's nice. And will you look at that face!

YOUNG MAN

Yes, it's quite good, isn't it? Clean-cut, midwest farm boy type, almost insultingly good-looking in a typically American way. Good profile, straight nose, honest eyes, wonderful smile . . .

GRANDMA

Yup. Boy, you know what you are, don't you? You're the American Dream, that's what you are. All those other people, they don't know what they're talking about. You . . . *you* are the American Dream.

YOUNG MAN

Thanks.

MOMMY

(*Off stage*)
Who rang the doorbell?

GRANDMA
(Shouting off-stage)
The American Dream!

MOMMY
(Off stage)
What? What was that, Grandma?

GRANDMA
(Shouting)
The American Dream! The American Dream! Damn it!

DADDY
(Off stage)
How's that, Mommy?

MOMMY
(Off stage)
Oh, some gibberish; pay no attention. Did you find Grandma's room?

DADDY
(Off stage)
No. I can't even find Mrs. Barker.

YOUNG MAN
What was all that?

GRANDMA
Oh, that was just the folks, but let's not talk about them, honey; let's talk about you.

YOUNG MAN
All right.

GRANDMA

Well, let's see. If you're not the van man, what are you doing here?

YOUNG MAN

I'm looking for work.

GRANDMA

Are you! Well, what kind of work?

YOUNG MAN

Oh, almost anything . . . almost anything that pays. I'll do almost anything for money.

GRANDMA

Will you . . . will you? Hmmmm. I wonder if there's anything you could do around here?

YOUNG MAN

There might be. It looked to be a likely building.

GRANDMA

It's always looked to be a rather unlikely building to me, but I suppose you'd know better than I.

YOUNG MAN

I can sense these things.

GRANDMA

There *might* be something you could do around here. Stay there! Don't come any closer.

YOUNG MAN

Sorry.

GRANDMA

I don't mean I'd *mind*. I don't know whether I'd mind, or not. . . . But it wouldn't look well; it would look just *awful*.

YOUNG MAN

Yes; I suppose so.

GRANDMA

Now, stay there, let me concentrate. What could you do? The folks have been in something of a quandary around here today, sort of a dilemma, and I wonder if you mightn't be some help.

YOUNG MAN

I hope so . . . if there's money in it. Do you have any money?

GRANDMA

Money! Oh, there's more money around here than you'd know what to do with.

YOUNG MAN

I'm not so sure.

GRANDMA

Well, maybe not. Besides, I've got money of my own.

YOUNG MAN

You have?

GRANDMA

Sure. Old people quite often have lots of money; more often than most people expect. Come here, so I can whisper to you . . . not too close. I might faint.

Oh, I'm sorry.

GRANDMA

It's all right, dear. Anyway . . . have you ever heard of that big baking contest they run? The one where all the ladies get together in a big barn and bake away?

YOUNG MAN

I'm . . . not . . . sure. . . .

GRANDMA

Not so close. Well, it doesn't matter whether you've heard of it or not. The important thing is—and I don't want anybody to hear this . . . the folks think I haven't been out of the house in eight years—the important thing is that I won first prize in that baking contest this year. Oh, it was in all the papers; not under my own name, though. I used a *nom de boulangère*; I called myself Uncle Henry.

YOUNG MAN

Did you?

GRANDMA

Why not? I didn't see any reason not to. I look just as much like an old man as I do like an old woman. And you know what I called it . . . what I won for?

YOUNG MAN

No. What did you call it?

GRANDMA

I called it Uncle Henry's Day-Old Cake.

YOUNG MAN

That's a very nice name.

GRANDMA

And it wasn't any trouble, either. All I did was go out and get a store-bought cake, and keep it around for a while, and then slip it in, unbeknownst to anybody. Simple.

YOUNG MAN

You're a very resourceful person.

GRANDMA

Pioneer stock.

YOUNG MAN

Is all this true? Do you want me to believe all this?

GRANDMA

Well, you can believe it or not . . . it doesn't make any difference to me. All *I* know is, Uncle Henry's Day-Old Cake won me twenty-five thousand smackerolas.

YOUNG MAN

Twenty-five thou—

GRANDMA

Right on the old loggerhead. Now . . . how do you like them apples?

YOUNG MAN

Love 'em.

GRANDMA

I thought you'd be impressed.

Money talks.

GRANDMA

Hey! You look familiar.

YOUNG MAN

Hm? Pardon?

GRANDMA

I said, you look familiar.

YOUNG MAN

Well, I've done some modeling.

GRANDMA

No . . . no. I don't mean that. You look familiar.

YOUNG MAN

Well, I'm a type.

GRANDMA

Yup; you sure are. Why do you say you'd do anything for money . . . if you don't mind my being nosy?

YOUNG MAN

No, no. It's part of the interview. I'll be happy to tell you. It's that I have no talents at all, except what you see . . . my person; my body, my face. In every other way I am incomplete, and I must therefore . . . compensate.

GRANDMA

What do you mean, incomplete? You look pretty complete to me.

I think I can explain it to you, partially because you're very old, and very old people have perceptions they keep to themselves, because if they expose them to other people . . . well, you know what ridicule and neglect are.

I do, child, I do.

Then listen. My mother died the night that I was born, and I never knew my father; I doubt my mother did. But, I wasn't alone, because lying with me . . . in the placenta . . . there was someone else . . . my brother . . . my twin.

Oh, my child.

We were identical twins . . . he and I . . . not fraternal . . . identical; we were derived from the same ovum; and in *this*, in that we were twins not from separate ova but from the same one, we had a kinship such as you cannot imagine. We . . . we felt each other breathe . . . his heartbeats thundered in my temples . . . mine in his . . . our stomachs ached and we cried for feeding at the same time . . . are you old enough to understand?

I think so, child; I think I'm nearly old enough.

I hope so. But we were separated when we were still
very young, my brother, my twin and I . . . inasmuch
as you can separate one being. We were torn apart . . .
thrown to opposite ends of the continent. I don't know
what became of my brother . . . to the rest of myself
. . . except that, from time to time, in the years that
have passed, I have suffered losses . . . that I can't explain. A fall from grace . . . a departure of innocence
. . . loss . . . loss. How can I put it to you? All right;
like this: Once . . . it was as if all at once my heart . . .
became numb . . . almost as though I . . . almost as
though . . . just like that . . . it had been wrenched
from my body . . . and from that time I have been unable to love. Once . . . I was asleep at the time . . . I
awoke, and my eyes were burning. And since that time
I have been unable to see anything, *anything*, with pity,
with affection . . . with anything but . . . cool disin-
terest. And my groin . . . even there . . . since one
time . . . one specific agony . . . since then I have not
been able to *love* anyone with my body. And even my
hands . . . I cannot touch another person and feel love.
And there is more . . . there are more losses, but it all
comes down to this: I no longer have the capacity to feel
anything. I have no emotions. I have been drained, torn
asunder . . . disemboweled. I have, now, only my person . . . my body, my face. I use what I have . . . I
let people love me . . . I accept the syntax around me,
for while I know I cannot relate . . . I know I must be
related *to*. I let people love me . . . I let people touch
me . . . I let them draw pleasure from my groin . . .
from my presence . . . from the fact of me . . . but,
that is all it comes to. As I told you, I am incomplete
. . . I can feel nothing. I can feel nothing. And so

. . . here I am . . . as you see me. I am . . . but this
. . . what you see. And it will always be thus.

GRANDMA

Oh, my child; my child.
> (*Long pause; then*)

I was mistaken . . . before. I don't know you from
somewhere, but I knew . . . once . . . someone very
much like you . . . or, very much as perhaps you were.

YOUNG MAN

Be careful; be very careful. What I have told you may
not be true. In my profession . . .

GRANDMA

Shhhhhh.
> (*The* YOUNG MAN *bows his head, in acquies-
> cence*)

Someone . . . to be more precise . . . who might have
turned out to be very much like you might have turned
out to be. And . . . unless I'm terribly mistaken . . .
you've found yourself a job.

YOUNG MAN

What are my duties?

MRS. BARKER

> (*Off stage*)

Yoo-hoo! Yoo-hoo!

GRANDMA

Oh-oh. You'll . . . you'll have to play it by ear, my dear
. . . unless I get a chance to talk to you again. I've got
to go into my act, now.

YOUNG MAN

But, I . . .

GRANDMA

Yoo-hoo!

MRS. BARKER

(*Coming through archway*)
Yoo-hoo . . . . oh, there you are, Grandma. I'm glad to see somebody. I can't find Mommy or Daddy.
(*Double takes*)
Well . . . who's this?

GRANDMA

This? Well . . . un . . . oh, this is the . . . uh . . . the van man. That's who it is . . . the van man.

MRS. BARKER

So! It's true! They *did* call the van man. They *are* having you carted away.

GRANDMA

(*Shrugging*)
Well, you know. It figures.

MRS. BARKER

(*To* YOUNG MAN)
How dare you cart this poor old woman away!

YOUNG MAN

(*After a quick look at* GRANDMA, *who nods*)
I do what I'm paid to do. I don't ask any questions.

80

MRS. BARKER

(*After a brief pause*)

Oh.

(*Pause*)

Well, you're quite right, of course, and I shouldn't meddle.

GRANDMA

(*To* YOUNG MAN)

Dear, will you take my things out to the van?

(*She points to the boxes*)

YOUNG MAN

(*After only the briefest hesitation*)

Why certainly.

GRANDMA

(*As the* YOUNG MAN *takes up half the boxes, exits by the front door*)

Isn't that a nice young van man?

MRS. BARKER

(*Shaking her head in disbelief, watching the* YOUNG MAN *exit*)

Unh-hunh . . . some things have changed for the better. I remember when I had *my* mother carted off . . . the van man who came for her wasn't anything near as nice as this one.

GRANDMA

Oh, did you have your mother carted off, too?

MRS. BARKER

(*Cheerfully*)
Why certainly! Didn't you?

GRANDMA

(*Puzzling*)
No . . . no, I didn't. At least, I can't remember. Listen dear; I got to talk to you for a second.

MRS. BARKER

Why certainly, Grandma.

GRANDMA

Now, listen.

MRS. BARKER

Yes, Grandma. Yes.

GRANDMA

Now listen carefully. You got this dilemma here with Mommy and Daddy . . .

MRS. BARKER

Yes! I wonder where they've gone to

GRANDMA

They'll be back in. Now, LISTEN!

MRS. BARKER

Oh, I'm sorry.

GRANDMA

Now, you got this dilemma here with Mommy and Daddy, and I think I got the way out for you.

(The YOUNG MAN *re-enters through the front door)*

Will you take the rest of my things out now, dear?

(To MRS. BARKER, *while the* YOUNG MAN *takes the rest of the boxes, exits again by the front door)*

Fine. Now listen, dear.

(She begins to whisper in MRS. BARKER's *ear)*

MRS. BARKER

Oh! Oh! Oh! I don't think I could . . . do you really think I could? Well, why not? What a wonderful idea . . . what an absolutely wonderful idea!

GRANDMA

Well, yes, I thought it was.

MRS. BARKER

And you so old!

GRANDMA

Heh, heh, heh.

MRS. BARKER

Well, I think it's absolutely marvelous, anyway. I'm going to find Mommy and Daddy right now.

GRANDMA

Good. You do that.

MRS. BARKER

Well, now. I think I will say good-by. I can't thank you enough.

(She starts to exit through the archway)

You're welcome. Say it!

MRS. BARKER

Huh? What?

GRANDMA

Say good-by.

MRS. BARKER

Oh. Good-by.
> (*She exits*)

Mommy! I say, Mommy! Daddy!

GRANDMA

Good-by.
> (*By herself now, she looks about*)

Ah me.
> (*Shakes her head*)

Ah me.
> (*Takes in the room*)

Good-by.
> (*The* YOUNG MAN *re-enters*)

GRANDMA

Oh, hello, there.

YOUNG MAN

All the boxes are outside.

GRANDMA
> (*A little sadly*)

I don't know why I bother to take them with me. They
don't have much in them . . . some old letters, a couple

84

of regrets . . . Pekinese . . . blind at that . . . the
television . . . my Sunday teeth . . . eighty-six years
of living . . . some sounds . . . a few images, a little
garbled by now . . . and, well . . .
> (*She shrugs*)
. . . you know . . . the things one accumulates.

Can I get you . . . a cab, or something?

Oh no, dear . . . thank you just the same. I'll take it
from here.

And what shall I do now?

Oh, you stay here, dear. It will all become clear to you.
It will be explained. You'll understand.

Very well.

> (*After one more look about*)
Well . . .

Let me see you to the elevator.

Oh . . . that *would* be nice, dear.
> (*They both exit by the front door, slowly*)

(*Enter* MRS. BARKER, *followed by* MOMMY *and* DADDY)

MRS. BARKER

. . . and I'm happy to tell you that the whole thing's settled. Just like that.

MOMMY

Oh, we're so glad. We were afraid there might be a problem, what with delays, and all.

DADDY

Yes, we're very relieved.

MRS. BARKER

Well, now; that's what professional women are for.

MOMMY

Why . . . where's Grandma? Grandma's not here! Where's Grandma? And look! The boxes are gone, too. Grandma's gone, and so are the boxes. She's taken off, and she's stolen something! Daddy!

MRS. BARKER

Why, Mommy, the van man was here.

MOMMY

(*Startled*)
The what?

MRS. BARKER

The van man. The van man was here.
(*The lights might dim a little, suddenly*)

MOMMY
(Shakes her head)
No, that's impossible.

MRS. BARKER
Why, I saw him with my own two eyes.

MOMMY
(Near tears)
No, no, that's impossible. No. There's no such thing
as the van man. There is no van man. We . . . we
made him up. Grandma? Grandma?

DADDY
(Moving to MOMMY*)*
There, there, now.

MOMMY
Oh Daddy . . . where's Grandma?

DADDY
There, there, now.
(While DADDY *is comforting* MOMMY, GRANDMA
comes out, stage right, near the footlights)

GRANDMA
(To the audience)
Shhhhhh! I want to watch this.
(She motions to MRS. BARKER *who, with a secret
smile, tiptoes to the front door and opens it.
The* YOUNG MAN *is framed therein. Lights up full
again as he steps into the room)*

Yes, sir! Yes, sirree! Now this is more like it. Now this is a great deal more like it! Daddy! Come see. Come see if this isn't a great deal more like it.

DADDY

I . . . I can see from here, Mommy. It does look a great deal more like it.

MOMMY

Yes, sir. Yes siree! Mrs. Barker, I don't know *how* to thank you.

MRS. BARKER

Oh, don't worry about that. I'll send you a bill in the mail.

MOMMY

What this really calls for is a celebration. It calls for a drink.

MRS. BARKER

Oh, what a nice idea.

MOMMY

There's some sauterne in the kitchen.

YOUNG MAN

I'll go.

MOMMY

Will you? Oh, how nice. The kitchen's through the archway there.

(*As the* YOUNG MAN *exits: to* MRS. BARKER)

He's very nice. Really top notch; much better than the other one.

MRS. BARKER

I'm glad you're pleased. And I'm glad everything's all straightened out.

MOMMY

Well, at least we know why we sent for you. We're glad that's cleared up. By the way, what's his name?

MRS. BARKER

Ha! Call him whatever you like. He's yours. Call him what you called the other one.

MOMMY

Daddy? What did we call the other one?

DADDY

(*Puzzles*)
Why . . .

YOUNG MAN

(*Re-entering with a tray on which are a bottle of sauterne and five glasses*)
Here we are!

MOMMY

Hooray! Hooray!

MRS. BARKER

Oh, good!

MOMMY

(Moving to the tray)

So, let's— Five glasses? Why five? There are only four of us. Why five?

YOUNG MAN

(Catches GRANDMA's *eye;* GRANDMA *indicates she is not there)*

Oh, I'm sorry.

MOMMY

You must learn to count. We're a wealthy family, and you must learn to count.

YOUNG MAN

I will.

MOMMY

Well, everybody take a glass.

(They do)

And we'll drink to celebrate. To satisfaction! Who says you can't get satisfaction these days!

MRS. BARKER

What dreadful sauterne!

MOMMY

Yes, isn't it?

(To YOUNG MAN, *her voice already a little fuzzy from the wine)*

You don't know how happy I am to see you! Yes sirree. Listen, that time we had with . . . with the other one. I'll tell you about it some time.

(Indicates MRS. BARKER*)*

After she's gone. She was responsible for all the trouble in the first place. I'll tell you all about it.
(*Sidles up to him a little*)
Maybe . . . maybe later tonight.

YOUNG MAN
(*Not moving away*)
Why yes. That would be very nice.

MOMMY
(*Puzzles*)
Something familiar about you . . . you know that? I can't quite place it. . . .

GRANDMA
(*Interrupting . . . to audience*)
Well, I guess that just about wraps it up. I mean, for better or worse, this is a comedy, and I don't think we'd better go any further. No, definitely not. So, let's leave things as they are right now . . . while everybody's happy . . . while everybody's got what he wants . . . or everybody's got what he thinks he wants. Good night, dears.

CURTAIN